Crown Jewel

of Fairmount Park

Belmont Mansion

Historic Home of the Peters Family

in

Philadelphia's West Fairmount Park

under the Stewardship

of

The American Women's Heritage Society, Inc

By Audrey R. J. Thornton

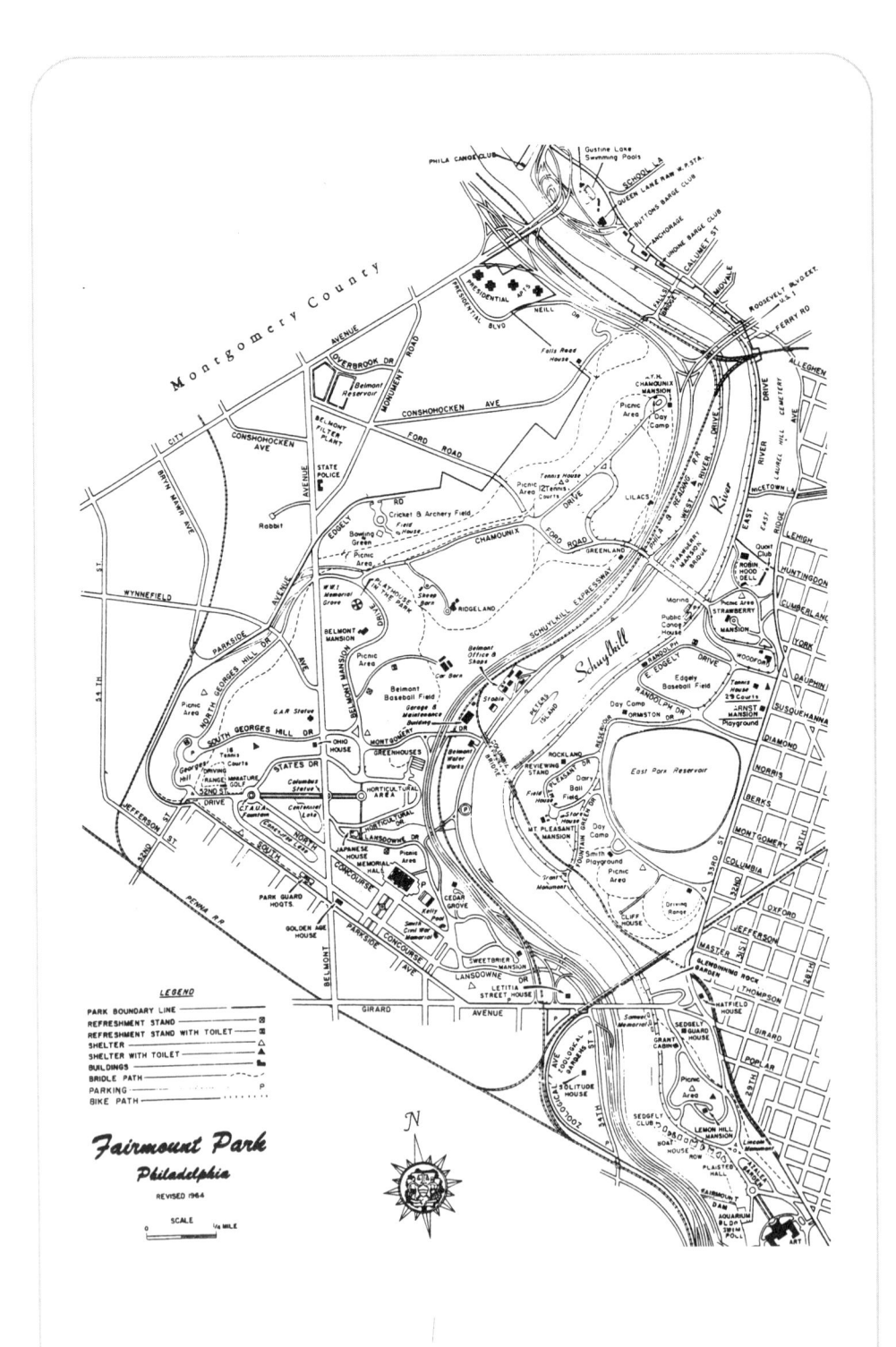

Figure 1 Map of Fairmount Park

Dedicated to my wonderful husband

Bernard Thornton, Sr

for his support, devotion, and dedication to
our many projects;
for his creative abilities,
his dependability.
His love is endless.

Contents

Acknowledgments

Mrs. Johnson-Thornton, President, American Women's Heritage Society, Inc.

Dr. Mary K. Dabney, Consulting Curator, Principal Research and Writing.

Olivia A. Butler, Student Matriculated her Doctorate in History Research at Temple University, conducted additional research.

Melba R. Guy. American Women's Heritage Society, Inc. Trustee Toni Nash, American Women's Heritage Society, Inc. Trustee actively contributed to this work.

Vanesse Lyod - Sgambati, President of the Literary, who provided the resources for publication

Ralph Peters, direct descendent of the original owners, Richard Peters, for his valuable suggestions.

Charles Blockson, Curator of the Blockson Afro-American Collection at Temple University, and Jeff Cohen, Bryn Mawr College, contributed comments in their areas of expertise.

Our gratitude goes to the staffs of the archives at the Historical Society of Pennsylvania, the University of Pennsylvania, and the Fairmount Park Commission for their valued assistance.

Introduction

Belmont Mansion is the oldest mansion in Fairmount Park and is the only mansion that sits on a plateau. Originally, a 400-acre property had been granted by William Penn in 1684 to John Boelsen and John Skutten. The property passed through several owners until 1742 when the widow of Daniel Jones sold it to William Peters, a prominent Philadelphia lawyer and loyalist.

In 1786, Richard Peters, William's son, also a successful lawyer and federal judge, resided here. In fact, the Peter's family was the only family to ever reside in the mansion.

The deed offered little guidance in identifying the builder of the original stone cottage house. It is believed that at the time of Peters' purchase of the property, the stone cottage was already built. The interior features of the stone cottage suggest it was built in the late 17th or early 18th century by Dutch or Swedish settlers.

The mansion evolved around the stone cottage and was built under the direction of William Peters. From 1745 to the 1760's, numerous additions were built (stair tower, main block, main house, brick farm houses). The living room or central room is noted for its ornamental plaster ceilings and exceptional woodwork, which is among the first in an American house. The musical instruments are intermingled with the Peters' coat of arms and crest.

In the early 1800's when the Peters family left the property, Belmont was a fine example of the early Georgian style of architecture. In 1867, it was purchased by the City of Philadelphia and incorporated into Fairmount Park. In the 1870's in preparation for the Centennial, the Park Commission attempted to turn Belmont into a restaurant, which resulted in a commercial disaster. Throughout the 1920's, it was a museum and playhouse. From the 1940's to 1970, restaurants were operated under several proprietors.

Left abandoned and unattended for 15 years, the Junior League opened it as a designer showcase in 1985. In 1986, the American Women's Heritage Society was formed for the purpose of restoring the Mansion and to preserve a valuable and historical landmark.

Belmont Mansion is exciting history about life, building a home, establishing one self in a new environment, politics, slavery, vision and foresight. The Crown Jewel of Fairmount Park relates to the history of the people who lived and worked there, who became a significant part of the history of Philadelphia.

We hope you will enjoy the history of a Historical House and how it affected many lives throughout four centuries.

REDISCOVERING BELMONT MANSION

THE AMERICAN WOMEN'S HERITAGE SOCIETY, INC.

Belmont Mansion is one of the first fully developed Palladian style villas in the American colonies. Its original design included one of the most extensive and earliest ornamental gardens to combine the formal and natural styles. During the Early American era, it served as a retreat for the Founding Fathers, George Washington, John Adams, Thomas Jefferson, and many more. Its owner, Judge Richard Peters was an active supporter of the abolition of slavery.

The American Women's Heritage Society is proud of their 15-year stewardship of Belmont Mansion and proud also to have initiated the Belmont Mansion Restoration Project. Phase I has completed and the restoration of the Belmont Mansion Historic House will be completed during Phase 2. Visitors to "The House on the Hill" have always enjoyed the view from atop the Belmont Plateau in West Fairmount Park along the Schuylkill River to the Philadelphia Skyline (Fig. 1). Throughout the history of Belmont Mansion, the house and grounds have been a show place history of one of the most historically and architecturally important colonial houses in America. You are invited to join us in exploring the history of one of the most historically and architecturally important colonial houses in America.

Figure 1a: Philadelphia Skyline from the Belmont Mansion

*Figure 2: Conjectural evolution of Belmont Mansion by Anthiony Ciasullo
and Peter A. Copp for Martin Jay Rosenblum & Associates*

Belmont Mansion in the Colonial Period

Among the 17th century Dutch and Swedish settlers of Philadelphia was Jan Boelsen, the first owner of the property around Belmont Mansion. The earliest record of the property lists it as jointly held since 1678 by Boelsen and Jan Schoeten. William Penn recognized their ownership of the property in 1684. They probably leased the land to tenant farmers. The only surviving farmhouse from that era may be the structure called Boelsen Cottage, located on the banks of the Schuylkill River near Peter's Island. Early in the 18th century, Boelsen's property was divided and sold to numerous small farmers who had emigrated from England. In 1742 William Peters, builder of Belmont Mansion, created his estate by purchasing their farms, at that time still far from the City of Philadelphia.

Belmont Cottage, the earliest building in the present Belmont Mansion Complex, is a unique example of an early 18th century farmhouse (Fig. 2). It was built as an independent structure before 1742 when William Peters bought the property. The cottage has a surviving asymmetrical roof (a two-story front sloping to a lower rear elevation) found in rural English houses. The original placements of the doors and windows on the facades were also asymmetrical. The asymmetry of the design stands in contrast to the strict symmetry of the later Belmont Mansion. The cottage's reconstructed interior layout, composed of a square divided into a hall and a parlor with corner fireplaces, was a composite of European house designs. It incorporates a mixture of building traditions from England, Germany, and Sweden, representing each of the early European settlers of the Delaware Valley.

William Peters, born in 1702, was an upper-class lawyer who moved from Liverpool, England to Philadelphia in 1739 (Fig. 3). His younger brother, Reverend Richard Peters, who had become Proprietary Secretary of Pennsylvania, overseeing land transactions for the Penn family, came four years earlier escaping a personal scandal. William also came to Philadelphia as a result of personal problems, leaving his wife, Elizabeth Bayley, and their four children in England. Income from his English land rents went to support her. In Philadelphia, Richard helped William obtain work as a lawyer and as an agent for the Penn family enforcing the collection of their Pennsylvania land rents. Later William attained the posts of Notary Public for Philadelphia, Prothonotary of the Superior Court, and Register of the Admiralty Court of Pennsylvania.

With the death of his father in 1742 and the illness of his wife, William gained control of his assets in England. This allowed him a substantial income. With these funds, he purchased a group of farms that he turned into a 200-acre country retreat on the English model. The small farmhouse, later known as the Belmont Cottage, already stood on the property at the time of the purchase. He also maintained a townhouse at Front and Pine in Philadelphia.

In Philadelphia, William met Mary Breintnall (Fig. 4), born in 1723 to David Breintnall, a leather artisan, and Susannah Shoemaker. They had been Quakers until her father was cast out of the Philadelphia Monthly Meeting apparently for drinking to excess. She was also the niece and heir of Mary Andrews, a relative of the Colonial Governor of New York.

Figure 3: Portrait of William Peters by John Wollaston, Historical Society of Pennsylvania

Figure 4:   Portrait of Mary Breintnall Peters by Robert Feke, Historical Society of Pennsylvania

William made the small farmhouse, later known as Belmont Cottage, a home for Mary Breintnall. Belmont Cottage was also the birthplace of their two sons, William, Jr. and Richard. To accommodate Mary and their children, William renovated the cottage, adding the brick addition and the three-sided bay. The brick addition was rebuilt in the mid-nineteenth century. At the same time, William Peters began the building of the Belmont Mansion after his own design. On the model of English country estates William conceived of Belmont Mansion as a suburban villa, providing an escape from the city. An amateur architect, he is also known to have provided designs for Cliveden, the Chew family country estate in Germantown. After the death of William's wife in England, Mary and William were married at Trinity Church in Oxford, Pennsylvania in 1744. Their sons were baptized at the same time. She was only twenty-one years old and he was forty-two.

Finished in 1745 according to the date stone, Belmont Mansion is one of the first fully developed Palladian style villa in the American colonies. Palladian style means in the style of Palladio, an Italian Renaissance architect. Palladio built suburban villas, which gave urban gentlemen a nearby place to restore the body and mind in a carefully planned "natural" landscape. These villas characteristically have a central hall, flanked by side chambers, just as seen at Belmont Mansion. Initially the staircase was a small winding one located on one side, but a central stair tower was added slightly later. Symmetry in architectural features is another important characteristic of the Palladian style. When viewing the interior walls in the central hall at Belmont Mansion, the visitor sees a symmetrical arrangement of fireplaces, doors, and windows (Fig. 5).

Following the model of English villa retreats, William transformed the farmland immediately surrounding the Mansion into ornamental gardens. For the colonies, the landscape design was one of the most extensive (nearly a mile long) and among the earliest of the "transitional" style. This style combined the geometric formality of 17th — early 18th century gardens with the informal "natural" landscapes becoming more popular in the later 18th century. A broad walk lined by cherry trees led from the Mansion to the river. From the rear of the Mansion, an axial gravel path led to a summer house and then on to an obelisk twenty-five feet high. The formal gardens to the rear of the Mansion were composed of a labyrinth of cedar and spruce hedges clipped to form pyramids, obelisks, and balls. Classical statuary (Apollo, Diana, and Mercury) and marble vases lay on one side, a vista cut through the hemlocks with a Chinese temple for a summerhouse on the other. The avenue of hemlocks remained a noted feature of the grounds for over 100 years.

By 1762, William Peters enlarged Belmont Mansion, adding separate but dependent buildings to each side of the Mansion connected by covered piazzas. In 1798 these structures were removed prior to renovations. He also added the existing stair tower in about 1765. In the stair tower and the central hall are preserved the earliest modeled plaster ceilings in America. The ceiling design reflects William's love of music. It is an original design composed of the arms of the Peters family with its motto *Sans Dieu Rien* (Without God Nothing), musical instruments, scallop shells, and floral garlands. It contains individual elements found in ceilings known from 18th century England and illustrated in William Jones's *The Gentlemen's or*

Figure 5 Belmont Mansion Central Hall

Belmont Mansion From Northeast, Circa 1871

Builder's Companion (1739). Similar plaster ceilings known from 18th century England are the work of traveling Italian plaster workers, who must have been brought to Belmont by William Peters.

William Peters demonstrated his love of the arts in many ways. He corresponded with Thomas Penn in England in order to encourage musicians to come to the colonies. He accepted landscape oil paintings in place of rents on his property in England. These paintings, along with family portraits, hung in the panels above the mantelpieces and in the stairwell. He also maintained a private library, importing books from England, and was a member of the Library Company of Philadelphia.

The interior of Belmont Mansion was, in part, outfitted with furnishings inherited from his wife's aunt Mary Andrews. Among these furnishings were a walnut desk and bookcase, a large mirror, paintings, bed and table linens, china and a silver tankard with the monogram of Edward Andrews, Governor of New York.

By 1767, the Belmont estate produced the largest income in Blockley Township. William used 64 acres surrounding the Mansion as a plantation, which included the ownership of two slaves. He rented the remaining 251 acres to farmers.

Correspondence between William and his brother Richard indicates that William was better at managing his property than he was at managing his children. When his twelve-year-old son William became too disruptive to continue his studies at the Academy, William sought his brother's help to place his son in an apprenticeship. For the rest of his life William Jr. was troubled by alcoholism and debt and was dependent on family members for support.

As a result of a corruption scandal in 1766, the elder William was obliged to resign the position of Secretary to the Land Office in which he had followed his brother. Reverend Richard Peters had become Rector of Christ Church. William was said to have exacted excess fees, accepted bribes, and engaged in land speculation.

The following year, William abandoned his American family and returned to England. He left the care of Belmont to his American wife, Mary, and their son, Richard. Mary remained in the Philadelphia area until her death in 1795 and managed her property with assistance from both her son and her husband's brother, the Reverend Richard Peters.

As a result, William's son Richard became close to the uncle for whom he was named. Richard's education no doubt benefited from his association with his uncle, who had attained a Doctorate in Divinity from Oxford in 1771. Richard surely had access to his uncle's private library.

Richard was known in later life for his warm and kindly wit. Perhaps he developed this talent through opposition to his experiences at the Academy of Philadelphia with his Latin teacher David Dove. Richard described Dove as "a sarcastical and ill-tempered doggereliser, and was called Dove ironically — for his temper was that of a hawk, and his pen was the beak of a falcon pouncing on innocent prey" (Watson 1899: 561).

Richard attended the College of Philadelphia (now the University of Pennsylvania), for which his uncle was at one time

President of the Board of Trustees. Ultimately, Richard Peters became a lawyer, like his father, and was admitted to the bar in 1763. His specialty in land titles and his knowledge of German led him to work in the western part of the Pennsylvania colony where his own family owned land and wished to promote settlement. Richard owed his first government appointment, as Register in the Court of Vice-Admiralty at Philadelphia, to the influence of his uncle.

Through his uncle's connections, Richard joined the Pennsylvania delegation, which in 1768 attended the Treaty with the Indians of the Six Nations at Fort Stanwix, New York. On that occasion, Richard was adopted into a Native American tribe. He was given the name Tegochtias, for a warrior who had been named after a bird brought back as a war trophy from the south. These bird feathers decorated the moccasins given to Richard at his naming ceremony. In reference to this occasion, Richard made one of his well-remembered jests. The Native Americans had given the name Onas, meaning quill, to William Penn. Richard claimed to prefer his own name, joking that he would "not be ashamed of it, when the great & good Penn was denominated, not a whole bird, but merely a Quill." In later life he contemplated with distress the fate of his Native American brothers. To Roberts Vaux (September 6, 1825, Historical Society of Pennsylvania, Peters Family Papers, vol. 12, p. 51), he wrote "My nation is reduced, as is all that Confederacy, to a mere squad, if not entirely annihilated; though at that time it [the confederacy] could bring 3000 warriors into the field. One race of Men seems destined to extinguish another; and, if so, the whites have amply fulfilled their destiny."

Figure 8 Watercolor of Belmont Mansion in 1816 by Joshua R. Watson

Figure 8a Watercolor of Belmont Mansion in 1816 by Joshua R. Watson

Belmont Mansion

in the

Early American Period

By the time of his uncle's death in 1776, Richard had assumed management of Belmont (Fig. 6). Coming of age in America without the influence of his loyalist English father, Richard joined the Associators for the military defense of Pennsylvania. Originally formed to protect Philadelphia shipping from the threat of French and Spanish privateers, the Association was not recognized by the Proprietary Government established by the Penn family and so membership was treason. With the outbreak of the American Revolution, Richard Peters became an American Revolutionary Army officer and ultimately Secretary of the Board of War.

In 1776 Richard Peters married Sarah Robinson at Christ Church in Philadelphia (Fig. 7). Her father, Thomas Robinson, was a Quaker who had immigrated from Ireland. In her youth Sarah had become a ward of General Anthony Wayne, to whom her father was related through marriage, after her father died in the French and Indian War in the 1760's.

The decision to marry at that tumultuous time may seem surprising but Richard had a special incentive. His uncle's will gave Richard the substantial sum of 2,000 pounds, conditional upon his marriage. Perhaps Richard's uncle wished to insure that Richard's family life began in a more conventional way than had William's.

Richard and Sarah made a happy couple despite the difficult circumstances of their early married life. In a letter to Richard on military affairs dated November 12, 1776 (Historical Society of Pennsylvania, Anthony Wayne Papers, vol. 1, p. 121), General Wayne reported also the happiness with which Sarah had written to him regarding her new life as Richard's wife.

Sarah's brother was also an American Revolutionary Army officer. According to legend, Sarah used a secret tunnel at the family home at Naaman's Creek near Claymont, Delaware to send out a message alerting nearby American Revolutionary Army soldiers of British officers visiting the house. As a result the British officers were caught by surprise and captured.

After the war, Richard was an elected official in the early American government, serving as Representative to Congress under the Articles of Confederation, Speaker of the Pennsylvania Assembly, and Pennsylvania State Senator. In later life, he recalled his experiences as a politician with some misgivings, claiming that he "served a long term of bondage to legislation; and was glad to get up my indentures." In recalling his success with the passage of the first bill for roads and navigation, he reported that he "was obliged to buy votes by a species of bribery — giving local advantages, for the attainment of the general Good. Although this smells strongly of corruption, yet it is not so bad as distributing offices to secure personal aggrandizement. Everything seems good or bad by comparison, more than intrinsic merit or culpability" (letter to Samuel Breck, March 11, 1819, University of Pennsylvania Miscellaneous Manuscripts Collection).

Figure 6:
Portrait of Judge Richard Peters
by Rembrandt Peale, collection of
Richard Peters, Charlottesville,
Virginia.

Figure 7:
Portrait of Sarah Robinson Peters,
collection

Nevertheless, Richard was a strong advocate for the American system of governance. Richard wrote (Knight 1847: 105):

Added to our situation as a new country, where much land is to be had for little money, our political arrangements contribute to our happiness, and to our moderate, but competent wealth. We have no princes, to indulge the grades more immediately beneath them, in their pleasures and their passions, that they may themselves be supported at the expense of the nation, in their schemes of ambition and luxury; no over-grown nobles, to wanton on the hard earnings of an oppressed yeomanry!

In 1792, he was appointed Judge of the District Court of the United States for Pennsylvania. Richard held the position for the rest of his life even though funding for federal positions was low, because a tax base for the United States government had not yet been established. In legal matters, Judge Peters was a Federalist who believed in a strong federal sovereignty and the need for the federal courts to have common law powers. Peters demonstrated his position when presiding over the Whiskey Rebellion trial in 1795. In this case, he held the men who had raised arms to oppose a federal excise tax on whiskey guilty of treason.

Following America's independence, Richard was instrumental in persuading the Church of England to ordain Episcopal bishops in the United States. Richard was himself a life-long member of the congregation at St. Peter's Church in Philadelphia. He was also one of the founders of Episcopal Academy.

Although Richard had long managed the property, he did not inherit Belmont until 1786 when William Peters died in England. At that time, Belmont was still outside the City of Philadelphia, in the area of Blockley Township. In the 1790s, Richard Peters removed the covered piazzas and dependent buildings that flanked the main house and replaced them with one-story wings off the central hall to house a parlor and a library (Fig. 8). These wings were removed between 1850 and 1870. In addition, in the 1790s, Richard raised the ground level in front of the house and added a columned porch to the front of the Mansion. In addition to the Mansion, the property included a spring house, wash house, ice house, and coach houses.

In 1787, Richard was among the first non-Quakers to join the Pennsylvania Society for the Abolition of Slavery. His interest in the welfare of African-Americans was already evident at the time of the American Revolution. As Captain of his battalion in the American Revolutionary Army, Richard had solicited funds for paying an African American musician for his service as a drummer. As a judge, Peters witnessed the injustice of the Fugitive Slave Act of 1793. This law allowed slave owners and bounty hunters to capture escaped slaves who sought freedom in Pennsylvania. Abuses of the law caused the kidnapping of freedmen. Peters urged the Pennsylvania Abolition Society to work at overturning the law. Letters between Peters and his friends and fellow judges express his opposition to the law.

Richard's opinions were no doubt influenced by his Quaker friend and neighbor, Judge William Lewis. Judge Lewis owned Somerton (now known as Strawberry Mansion), just across the Schuylkill River from Belmont Mansion. Judge Lewis wrote the Act for the Gradual Abolition of Slavery in Pennsylvania. This act, passed in 1780, was the first law abolishing slavery.

As a judge, Richard found irreconcilable differences between the Fugitive Slave Act and normal judicial procedures. Expressing his opposition to the law in a letter to the Pennsylvania Abolition Society (December 31, 1816, Historical Society of Pennsylvania, Papers of the Pennsylvania Abolition Society #7-291), he wrote:

The deficits of this provision, without the experience we all have of their oppressive operation, are sufficiently apparent. The section isolates one of the fundamental principles of the administration of justice; a principle which in every other part of our code of laws is held sacred; in as much as it makes evidence, affidavits taken ex parte, and in the absence of the person who is to be affected by them; and thus authorizes the decision of a judge or magistrate against the liberty of a fellow man upon allegations which he had no opportunity to contradict; and the witnesses in support of which he was not permitted to confront or interrogate. If in a controversy about an inanimate object, or in support of a claim to an animal, evidence of this kind were offered and claimed to be relied on; it would be rejected at once and would not be heard. ....that upon ex parte and illegal testimony, a magistrate of the lowest grade may deliver an individual to all the sufferings of slavery and authorize his being dragged in irons from a place where he might have resided for years in the enjoyment of his liberty; in the midst of his family, whose only stay he may be; to a distant state, and there at once handed over to the charge of a merciless overseer.

In the same letter, Richard Peters also argued for the necessity of time limits on the period during which claim can be made on a fugitive slave. As he describes the resulting treatment of fugitive slaves as unjustly harsh, he makes clear that his opposition to the law was also clearly based on moral grounds. He wrote:

In fancy may have grown into manhood and old age may have come on; the interval between the time when the slave may have deserted the service of his master, or have been carried from it by his fugitive pursuit, and that at which he is claimed, may have extended to the usual length of the life of a man; and during this time the fugitive from labor may have become a husband and a father; and may have forgotten in the ties thus formed, and in the happiness they have produced the existence of a right to call him back to bondage. None of these circumstances; no length of time will avail; and, if discovered, he may be torn from all his enjoyments — from his home — his family and his habitation, and condemned to unendurable slavery. Ought this thing to be? Do not nature and justice call for their prohibition?

At home, Richard Peters acted on his convictions. Cornelia Wells was an African-American slave purchased and immediately freed, along with her daughter, by Richard Peters in 1811. Cornelia served a three-year indenture as cook to the Peters family at Belmont. On completion of her indenture, Richard gave her 30 dollars as a present. Then she moved to the Boelsen Cottage, at that time nicknamed "Pig's Eye," on the banks of the Schuylkill River within the Belmont estate and worked for wages as their washerwoman until she died in 1830.

She also ran an informal tavern there, selling spruce beer and horse-shaped ginger cakes.

In 1819 Richard Peters witnessed the debate in the United States Congress over the admission of Missouri as a state permitting slave ownership. Again, Peters organized his colleagues in Pennsylvania to oppose this expansion of slavery. In a letter to Roberts Vaux (February 17, 1819, Vaux Papers, Historical Society of Pennsylvania), Richard expressed his fear that the senators from Pennsylvania were conceding to the advocates of slavery by agreeing to the Missouri Compromise. Richard hoped to excite his fellow antislavery activists in the Pennsylvania Abolition Society to make their opposition felt by the passage of a resolution in the Pennsylvania State legislature and through the publication of newspaper articles.

Regarding plans for colonizing slaves in Africa, Richard thought that the concept had merit but that the immediate plans for achieving it were inadequate. In another letter to Roberts Vaux (February 12, 1820, Vaux Papers, Historical Society of Pennsylvania), he wrote that he regarded it "in the feeble hands in which it is placed impossible. The work is too great for them to accomplish. But when the time shall arrive that it ought to be undertaken, all the support it will require ought to be furnished to it."

At the time of his death, the members of the bar adopted a resolution in memory of Judge Peters that recognized his concerns for social justice by stating "No suitor was denied or delayed justice. The poor and humble were protected in their rights, and wrong-doers, of whatever class, were restrained and punished." (Scharf and Westcott 1884: 1530).

After inheriting Belmont upon his father's death in 1786, Richard continued to live in the urban center of Philadelphia for much of the year due to the difficulties of travel between Belmont and the city.

Richard sponsored the construction of the Schuylkill Permanent Bridge at Market Street. During the Revolutionary War Richard, with the aid of General Israel Putnam, had first designed and organized the construction of a temporary floating bridge at Market Street, using ship carpenters' floating stages. The Permanent Bridge, a covered wooden bridge, created continuous access between Philadelphia and its western suburbs, including Belmont. Building materials for the bridge's stone foundations were quarried on the Belmont estate. Upon its completion in 1804, Richard began to live all year at Belmont.

As President of the Philadelphia Society for the Promotion of Agriculture, Richard Peters was an early scientific agriculturist, turning Belmont into a model experimental farm. Recognizing the need for America to become economically self-sufficient after the American Revolution, Richard promoted scientific agriculture by writing and publishing articles on his improvements in agricultural practices. He experimented with the use of lime from the estate's limekilns to increase the fertility of the land. His publication of this work led him to become the first American to publish the scientific results of an agricultural experiment. On Belmont's front lawn, Peters kept flocks of sheep specially breed for the purpose of developing the American wool industry. He planted orchards and introduced new crops for feeding livestock. He experimented with the use of salt as a fertilizer, strewing stripes of varying quantities in the grass.

Richard's agricultural research was greatly valued by George Washington. Washington chose Richard to be his correspondent for Pennsylvania for a study on the state of agriculture in America in 1791. Richard concluded that farming, as a business, required too great an investment to be profitable in comparison to other businesses. Laborers, however, fared well because farm labor for hire was in short supply due to the opportunity for farmers to acquire their own land on the western frontier. As a result, Richard concluded that "our common people are better fed and clothed than in any other part of the world" (Knight 1847: 85). Richard explained the American family farm system where farmers owned their farm and hired little help. According to Richard, in the absence of slave labor, "the farmer and his family do the greater portion of the work of their farms within themselves. This is the reason why they can get forward and live well" (Knight 1847: 86).

Richard's interests extended beyond farming to other areas of environmental science. The Belmont Estate included Peters Island in the middle of the Schuylkill River. Richard leased Peters Island to shad and herring fishermen. After the building of dams ended the migration of shad into the Schuylkill River, Richard sought to introduce species of fish suited to closed water environments (Notice to be published in the Daily Advertiser by Richard Peters, April 28, 1822, University of Pennsylvania Manuscript Collection 92, Philadelphia Society for Promoting Agriculture Papers, Box 3, Folder 152, Item 4).

At the end of the Revolutionary War, Henry Steiner, a German redemptioner, was brought by Richard Peters to Belmont as a gardener, especially to maintain the fruit trees. Although

Steiner became disabled through work-related accidents in 1802, Richard kept him on until Steiner's death in 1827 with a small wage, so that he would not become a pauper.

In 1804 Richard's wife Sarah died at Belmont Mansion, which they had recently made their year-round home. In his prayer book (Fairmount Park Commission Archives, Belmont Mansion History File), Richard wrote:

But no words can express my Sense of her Worth & Virtues. These should be imitated by her children & their Descendants while they reverence her Memory, & gratefully recollect her parental Love & unremitted Affection; which ceased only with her Life; never having been abated for a Moment, 'till Death deprived us of what we held most dear. She died at Belmont; the Scene of long & uninterrupted Felicity...

Admiration for Sarah extended also to Richard's circle of friends. In his letter of condolence to Richard (December 23, 1806; Historical Society of Pennsylvania, Peters Family Papers, vol. 10, p. 113), Benjamin Rush wrote: "Dear Dear Woman! — Polite as if at Courts She had always been And Good — as if the World She had never seen."

After Sarah's death their unmarried daughter Sally managed the household at Belmont for her father until his death in 1828. The women of the house, Sarah and later Sally, managed the household by overseeing the work of servants. Indentured servants, like Cornelia Wells, performed the actual work of cooking and cleaning.

In 1810, when only Richard and his daughter Sally resided at Belmont, he employed six servants (cook, washerwoman, housemaid, house boy, coachman, and gardener) and a farm hand. The farmland was worked by additional tenant farmers.

Household duties were very labor intensive. Food preparation included processing their own farm products as well as cooking and serving them. Richard claims to have brewed excellent family beer for many years. A large dairy farm also operated on the estate. He had less success with beekeeping.

Entertaining in the home was the center of social life (Fig. 9). Visitors were attracted by the ornamental gardens created by Richard's father William and the scenic views along the river towards Philadelphia. Richard's experimental model farm also attracted visitors to Belmont. Through his political connections, Richard hosted many of the Founding Fathers of America: George Washington, Marquis de Lafayette, Baron von Steuben, John Adams, Thomas Jefferson, and James Madison. At one time, there stood on the grounds at Belmont a Spanish chestnut tree planted by Washington and a white walnut tree planted by

Figure 9 George Washington visiting Belmont Mansion

Lafayette. Frequent visits were also made by the leaders of Philadelphia: John Bartram, Benjamin Franklin, Robert Morris, John Penn, and David Rittenhouse.

Among his peers, Richard was known for his wit, characterized by comical anecdotes and puns. Marquis de Chastellux, in the journal of his travels in America, recounts a dinner in 1780 at which Richard entertained the guests with an original bawdy song (Rice 1963: 176). One visitor to Richard's model farm complained about the run-down appearance of the gate and fences. Richard replied, "How can you expect me to attend to all these things when my time is so taken up in telling others how to farm?" On the occasion of Lafayette's visit in 1824, one young man declared to those present, "Sir, although we were not born to partake of your Revolutionary hardships, yet we mean, should our country be attacked, to tread in the shoes of our brave forefathers." "No, no," cried Richard, "that you can never do, because your fathers fought barefooted."

Richard's daughter Sally was hostess to gatherings of well-educated women. She participated in literary and religious women's groups and was an advocate of useful work for women. In remembrance of Sally upon her death (Black 1904: 130), it was written that she was "possessed of a great natural vivacity and of a vigorous intellect, highly cultivated, she was the life of her social circle."

A sense of Richard's wealth can be obtained from a review of the expenses he recorded in his daybook for the year 1816. In that year he spent $ 2,976.96. At that time, an unskilled or semi-skilled laborer earned less than ten percent of that amount, only $ 250 per year. Richard's greatest category of expenditure (25% of his annual expenses) was for building work, including carpentry, masonry, plastering, painting, and papering, at a total of $ 740.50. Household expenses made up nineteen percent of his annual expenses, costing $ 546.36. These expenses included wages for housekeepers and purchases of furnishings such as new china and bedding as well as consumables such as firewood, candles, and ice. Food (beef, grains, sugar, tea, coffee, and especially wine) cost $ 446.70 (15%). Farm labor, livestock, and seeds totaled $ 389.16 (13%). Richard paid $ 300 (10%) interest on debt. Taxes were only $ 102.19 (3%). Also relatively little was spent on clothing ($ 58.86 or 2%) and transportation ($ 83.22 or 3%). Other incidental expenses included pew rent, newspaper subscriptions, and postage.

Portrayal of Cornelia Wells

Colonial 18th Century Costumes

Figure 9: View and details of Belmont Mansion, to Dining Pavillion erected 1876 and demolished 1888.

Belmont Mansion

in the

Early Industrial Period

Judge Richard Peters died in 1828 at the age of eighty-four. He left his estate, including Belmont Mansion, equally to his three children, Ralph, Richard Jr., and Sally. Earlier in life, he had expressed his opinion that the American system of equality in inheritance law was preferable to the European practice of leaving everything to the first-born son. Management of the estate was then turned over to Richard Jr. by his siblings. Richard Jr. was a lawyer who resided in Philadelphia. He also spent part of the year in Washington D.C. where he served as the Official Reporter to the United States Supreme Court. Although Richard Jr. never lived at Belmont Mansion, he controlled the use of the property until his death in 1848.

Richard Jr. increased the commercial development of Belmont begun late in his father's life. Richard Jr. was a member of the Pennsylvania Society for the Promotion of Internal Improvements that sponsored a trip to Europe by William Strickland in 1825 to study canals, railways, roads, and bridges. Based in part on Strickland's recommendation, the Columbia and Philadelphia Railroad was built in 1828 across the area between the mansion and the Schuylkill River. Just 200 feet from the mansion ran an inclined plane with a steam-driven cable system for pulling railroad cars up the hill from the bridge across the river (Fig. 10). The property was divided into several small farms rented to tenant farmers. Belmont's stone quarries and

Figure 10a Hotel down at the Schuylkill river erected by Richard Peters, Jr., 1866

Figure 10 View from the head of the inclined plane circa 1850

limekilns produced building materials for sale. In 1829, Belmont Cottage Hotel was constructed on the banks of the Schuylkill River alongside the Columbia and Philadelphia Railroad Bridge. This was the earliest commercial hospitality use of the property.

Although he had followed in his father's footsteps by becoming a lawyer, Richard Jr. did not depend on his father's connections and influence to attain positions. Moreover, father and son did not always agree on matters of family business. Judge Peters complained that Richard Jr. should be sponsoring his brother Ralph for a position in the Custom House instead of someone outside the family. They also disagreed about the value of making improvements on family property in western Pennsylvania for attracting settlers.

Despite his independence in other matters, Richard Peters, Jr. did follow his father's interest in fair treatment for African Americans. As a lawyer practicing in Philadelphia, Richard Jr. represented the African Episcopal Church of St. Thomas in a legal case concerning the handling of the church's financial accounts against Joseph Randolph in 1820. Richard Peters, Jr. himself had been brought up as a member of St. Peter's Episcopal Church. The documents indicate that Richard Jr. had personal interaction with the members of the Church, who served as witnesses in the case. One of the founders of the African Episcopal Church of St. Thomas had been Absalom Jones, a leader in protesting the kidnapping of free blacks. Also among the documents, no doubt read by Richard Jr., was the *Act of Incorporation, Causes and Motives, of the African Episcopal Church of Philadelphia* (Philadelphia 1810: 16) which eloquently described the trials and aspirations of African Americans in

Philadelphia at the time:

> And we are now encouraged through the grace and divine assistance of God opening the hearts of our white friends and brethren, to encourage us to arise out of dust and shake ourselves, and throw off that servile fear, that the habit of oppression and bondage trained us up in. And in meekness and fear we would desire to walk in liberty where with Christ has made us free.

> We, ... , have gone forward to erect a house for the glory of God, and our mutual advantage to meet in for edification and social religious worship. And more particularly to keep an open door for those of our race, who may be induced to assemble with us, but would not attend divine worship in other places; ....

Later, in 1842, as the Official Reporter to the United States Supreme Court, Richard Jr. published the legal case Prigg v. Pennsylvania. This decision upheld the imprisonment of an agent for taking a fugitive slave without a court certificate for removal. The case stimulated Underground Railroad activity in Pennsylvania by making the Fugitive Slave Act ineffective. Based on his father's previous experiences handling fugitive slave cases for the federal courts in Pennsylvania, Richard Jr. would have been well aware of the implications of this case.

As a result, fugitive slaves from Virginia and Maryland were considered free when they crossed the Susquehanna River to Columbia, Pennsylvania. There they were aided by the African-American lumber merchant William Whipper. Whipper sent them towards Philadelphia aboard lumber cars on the Columbia and Philadelphia Railroad.

Approaching Philadelphia, the Columbia and Philadelphia Railroad crossed the Schuylkill River at Belmont. The trains had to negotiate the inclined plane directly in front of Belmont Mansion. This would give fugitive slaves a chance to disembark from the railroad lumber cars and escape to the river. Peter's Island, offshore from the Boelsen Cottage in the Schuylkill River, would have made an excellent hiding place. Previously the island had been rented to shad fishermen. The Boelsen Cottage might have provided another refuge which exists today on the West River Drive.

Former tenants of Belmont Mansion suggested that an underground passageway ran from Belmont towards the river, echoing the tale of a similar escape tunnel at Sarah Robinson Peters' family home in Delaware. Archaeological research around Belmont Mansion shows that early 20th century changes in the landscape disturbed any original nineteenth century features, so any tunnel that existed may now be gone.

Belmont Mansion, commanding the view down to the river, was well situated for use by the Underground Railroad. The Peters family was sympathetic to the plight of escaped slaves but, as officials of the court, Judge Peters and his son could not have direct involvement in the Underground Railroad. Still, knowing the feelings of the Peters family, any of the numerous tenant farmers, servants, and freed slaves living at Belmont might have come to the aid of the fugitive slaves.

The publication of Prigg v. Pennsylvania by Richard Jr. and the resulting expansion of the Underground Railroad did not go unnoticed by Southern politicians who supported slavery.

Shortly after its publication, Richard Jr. was replaced in his position as Reporter to the U.S. Supreme Court at the insistence of a judge from the South. In a letter to Richard Jr. from Charles Sumner (February 2, 1843, Richard Peters Correspondence, Cadwalader Collection, Historical Society of Pennsylvania, vol. 2, p. 106), Sumner wrote: "I lose no time in expressing to you my mortification & chagrin, that you should have been the victim of such hasty, disingenuous, & unjust treatment, as it now seems, you have suffered. ... Perhaps political services claim even your office, the demon of party has entered the sacred precincts, where Marshall once presided with such serenity & justice." A letter to Richard Jr. from Sarah McLean (August 12, 1846, Richard Peters Correspondence, Cadwalader Collection, Historical Society of Pennsylvania, vol. 2, pp. 150-151) indicates how Southern politicians tried to ruin the Washington careers of those identified as Abolitionists. Mrs. McLean appealed to Richard Jr. for advice regarding the negative impact her public service work for the education of free people of color in Ohio was having on the career of her husband, Judge McLean.

After the death of Richard Peters Jr. in 1848 at age 84, trustees for the Peters family heirs were appointed to manage the property. For a short time they converted Belmont Mansion into a commercial resort. The construction of the third floor, rebuilding and extension of the brick addition, and replacement of the front porch have been attributed to this time. Elements of the pleasure gardens created by William Peters, such as an avenue of hemlocks draped with English ivy, were still preserved, according to A. J. Downing (1844: 31-32).

Belmont Mansion

in

Fairmount Park

The Fairmount Park Commission purchased the Belmont Estate in 1868. Fairmount Park was created to preserve the quality of the water supplied to City of Philadelphia residents by reducing industrial development along the Schuylkill River. With the acquisition of Belmont Mansion, the Commission bought out the Belmont Oil Company, established in 1864 within the estate (near the Boelsen Cottage) to refine oil.

The Fairmount Park Commission decided to lease out Belmont Mansion as a restaurant, just as had the trustees for the Peters family after the death of Richard Peters, Jr. Numerous "improvements" were made, including the creation of roads and paths and the construction of the Dining Pavilion. The Dining Pavilion was designed to serve as a place for shelter and "temperate" (non-alcoholic) refreshments. Open-air concerts were also held there once a week during the summer. These changes significantly altered the setting of the historic Belmont Mansion in its surrounding landscape. Weekend visitors to the newly created park often arrived by steamboats stopping at the Belmont landing on the Schuylkill River

Belmont Mansion was leased to restaurateur Adolph Proskauer. Proskauer previously had managed his own restaurants in Philadelphia and Cape May. At Proskauer's prompting, the large (180' x 40') Dining Pavilion was built to the southwest of the Mansion in 1871 (Fig. 11). A reception for

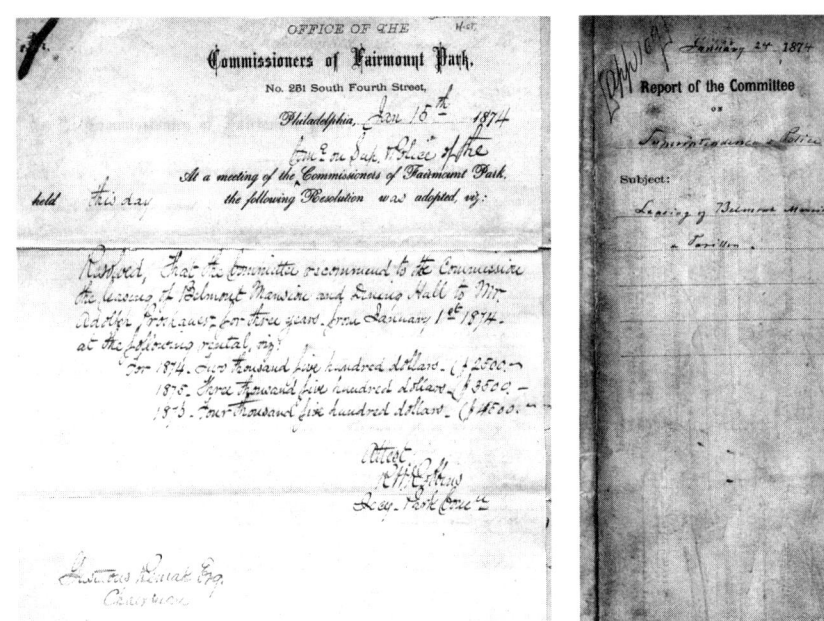

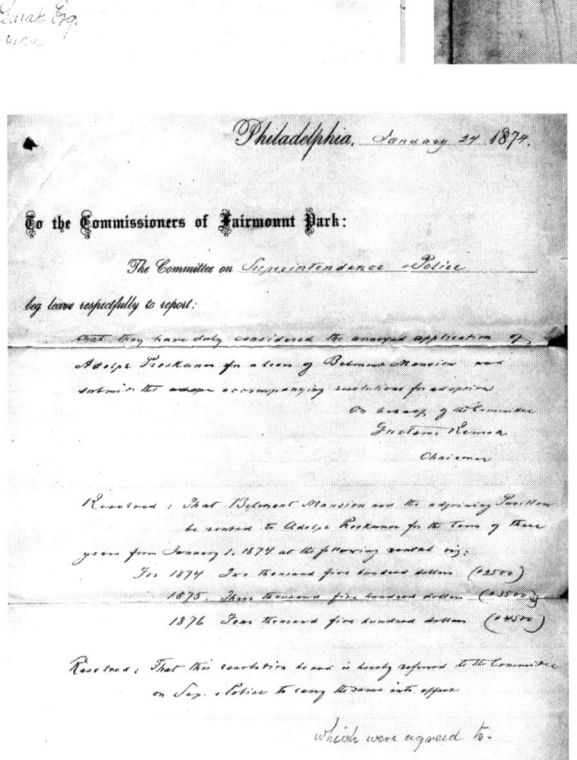

Figure 11: Fairmount Park Comission Lease, 1874

the Grand Duke Alexis of Russia was the inaugural event for the Dining Pavilion. Its design by Hermann Schwarzmann included a Swiss Chalet style exterior and interior "Pompeiian" style wall paintings. Schwarzmann was a German immigrant who later served as the primary designer of the buildings and grounds for the Centennial Exposition of 1876 and became Chief Engineer of Design for Fairmount Park. An annex connecting the pavilion to the cottage and its brick addition was added for the Centennial Exposition in 1876. This annex was removed in 1888 and replaced by the kitchen wing that has become the banquet hall today.

Newspaper articles, in connection with the Centennial Exposition of 1876, show that the historical significance of the Mansion itself and the need to preserve it was recognized even then. Ironically, competition from dining facilities at Philadelphia's Centennial Exposition of 1876 drove Proskauer out of business.

Public entertainment at Belmont Mansion continued into the 1890s and the early 20th century. Belmont Mansion was the desirable location it is today as part of Fairmount Park because of the immediately surrounding lawns and woods and the magnificent view. Boating parties on the river and walking parties in the park dined at the Mansion. In 1902, Belmont Mansion was the site for one of the first demonstrations of a radio broadcast. From 1889 to 1931, next to the kitchen stood two octagonal gazebos connected by a covered walkway, which together formed the Music Pavilion. Interest in restoring Belmont Mansion to its colonial appearance was revived during the Sesqui-Centennial Exhibition of 1926, when the site was

Figure 11a: Top - 1916 Music Pavillion - Bottom 1916 Dining Hall

used for theatrical performances. Afterwards Fritz Pflug operated a restaurant at Belmont Mansion. In 1935 a fire caused serious damage to the roof of the brick addition to the Mansion. Then Belmont Mansion suffered from a period of abandonment.

The Dining Pavilion was demolished in 1941. During the Second World War, Belmont Plateau was occupied by the 722nd Military Police Battalion under the Third Service Command. By 1943, 599 military personnel were housed in barracks built there. For two weeks in 1944, 6,000 military personnel were stationed in the Belmont Cantonment (also known as the Fairmount Park Cantonment). Their presence was in response to the labor problems in the Philadelphia Transit Company. In 1946 the property reverted to Fairmount Park, all military buildings were removed, and the entire area regraded. In 1946 Belmont Plateau was a candidate to be the home site of the United Nations, before it moved to New York.

After the war, Belmont Mansion was again the site of a restaurant, operated by Carl Mai from 1948 until 1955 and then by Charles and Helen Sigel. In 1954, the Playhouse-in-the-Park was built behind Belmont Mansion. Due to abandonment of the building, the Playhouse-in-the-Park was demolished by the City of Philadelphia in 1998. In 1963, Don Battles took over the management of a restaurant at Belmont Mansion. Then Belmont once again stood vacant.

Figure 12: Belmont Mansion Cottage, 1839

Figure 12a: Belmont Mansion, 1998

Belmont Mansion

and

The American Women's Heritage Society

The American Women's Heritage Society was founded as a volunteer organization in November 1986 for the purpose of maintaining and restoring historic Belmont Mansion (Fig. 12). Earlier in the spring of 1986 the cosmetic appearance of the interior of Belmont Mansion had been partially renovated to be a Designer Showhouse sponsored by the Junior League of Philadelphia. The Mansion had previously endured numerous additions and alterations for use as a restaurant and suffered from deferred maintenance and abandonment. The Society was formed as a non-profit historic preservation organization, the first organization to operate Belmont Mansion primarily as a historic site.

The American Women's Heritage Society under the leadership of Audrey R. Johnson-Thornton, who serves as the Society's President and Executive Director. Mrs. Johnson-Thornton was encouraged to organize a group of African-American women to manage Belmont Mansion by Mrs. Joseph Gembala, President of the Committee of 1926 that managed Strawberry Mansion. Mrs. Johnson-Thornton has extensive background in organizational management from her leadership positions with numerous non-profit organizations and from her service as a City Commissioner. Through her guidance, the Society acquired the lease for Belmont Mansion from the Fairmount Park Commission and obtained Federal income tax

Figure 13: Volunteers landscaping at Belmont Mansion

Figure 13a: Volunteers at Belmont Mansion

exempt status as a non-profit organization.

The American Women's Heritage Society is the only African-American women's organization to administer a historic mansion in Fairmount Park. Its three hundred members are comprised of a cross section of professional, business, and community leaders. These members serve as docents, providing historical tours of Belmont Mansion to the public (Fig. 13). Belmont Mansion is the only historic mansion in Fairmount Park that is open to the public six days a week throughout the year (closed Monday). Society members have raised the funds to purchase all the furnishings and equipment used in the Belmont Mansion Complex.

By the end of the first year of operation, it became clear that the minimal membership fees alone would not provide adequate funds for the maintenance of the Mansion. Unlike some of the other historic houses in Fairmount Park, Belmont Mansion has no maintenance endowment from the descendants of its original owners. Also the City of Philadelphia provides no operating support for Belmont Mansion. Maintenance of Belmont Mansion is completely dependent on the ability of the American Women's Heritage Society to earn income and obtain contributions. After serious consideration, the Society decided to rent the facility by advance reservation for private parties, weddings, conferences, and as a meeting place for social and cultural organizations. Today, this non-profit historic preservation organization raises funds from a combination of membership fees, admissions, rentals, grants, and donations.

The American Women's Heritage Society has succeeded

in drawing attention to the historical and architectural importance of Belmont Mansion. In a 1987 *Assessment of Ten Historic Structure in Fairmount Park* considered to be at risk, Belmont Mansion was singled out as the most significant structure studied and among the most important in Fairmount Park. This work was followed by a complete historical study and architectural analysis by Martin Jay Rosenblum & Associates published as the *Belmont Mansion Historic Structures Report* in 1992.

On this basis, the restoration of Belmont Mansion became in 1994 the first major project of the Fairmount Park Historic Preservation Trust (Figs. 14-23). The Fairmount Park Historic Preservation Trust was created by City Council in 1993 to provide management and capital funding for historic properties in Fairmount Park. Unfortunately, the Trust did not have the firsthand experience of occupying and operating these properties. It lacked the long-term understanding of the historic houses possessed by the members of the house volunteer organizations like the American Women's Heritage Society.

The $1.3 million Restoration Project funded by the City of Philadelphia, The Pew Charitable Trusts, and the William Penn Foundation brings Belmont Mansion closer to its original eighteenth century appearance. Centuries of alterations to Belmont Mansion mean that full restoration to its eighteenth century appearance is impossible. Phase 1 of the Restoration Project facilitates the adaptive reuse of the buildings adjacent to Belmont Mansion as a Multi-faceted Arts Center for exhibitions and performances as well as a facility for events that generate income for the maintenance of the Mansion. Simultaneously, archaeological and historical landscape research was carried out.

Figure 14: Belmont Mansion complex exterior during restoration

Figure 15: Belmont complex interior during restoration

Figure 16: Belmont Mansion complex exterior renovations

Figure 17: Belmont Mansion complex exterior renovations

The scope of the Restoration Project exceeded the original plans for Belmont projected at the time the Society took over its management in 1986. The discovery of significant structural problems had added to the complexity of the Restoration Project. The entire Mansion needs internal structural supports to hold up the weight of the upper stories and roof. The eighteenth-century modeled plaster ceiling is in danger of collapse.

The supervision of the Restoration Project at Belmont Mansion was challenging for all the parties involved. Over the three-and-one-half year period beginning with the allocation of funds and ending with the completion of Phase 1 of the Restoration Project, members of the Society's Board consulted with architects, engineers, and contractors to insure that the Restoration Project would fulfill the needs of the Society to operate both Belmont Mansion as a historic site and the Belmont Mansion Complex as a facility suitable for generating income from rentals. As a result many changes to the original restoration plans were authorized. The Belmont Mansion Complex, which includes both the pre-1742 Belmont Cottage, which is the oldest structure at the site, and the renovated 20th century additions, was detached from the Mansion. This split between the Complex and the Mansion has separated the area used for events from the core of the historic Mansion. Funding restrictions ultimately limited the extent of the kitchen and office facilities.

Thanks to the dedication of the American Women's Heritage Society, the Belmont Mansion Restoration Project is continuing despite a shortfall of funds from the Fairmount Park Commission for the completion of Phase 2. The Society continues to work with City Council, the Fairmount Park

Commission, and funding agencies to obtain the resources for completing the Restoration Project. As part of action, this group will go far. The community support and diversity is already a foundation for the Society and the site it maintains. This kind of support can spread, grow and set examples for other museum organizations which still remain closed and indifferent to the communities around them.

Upon completion of Phase 1 of the Restoration Project in June 1997, the Society returned to the Belmont Mansion Complex where it holds exhibits, performances, and events open to the public. When Phase 2 of the Restoration Project is completed, the Society will once again open Belmont Mansion to the public as a historic house museum.

Through the Society, Belmont Mansion has also become an interpretive and educational center for the history and culture of African-Americans and women. The Society seeks to expose the African-American community to the fine arts (literature, art, dance, and music) as well as build bridges of communication and interaction among the various ethnic communities in Philadelphia (Fig. 25). Belmont Mansion also serves as a site for wedding receptions, private parties, and meetings of civic and cultural organizations. Weddings at Belmont Mansion are memorable events that inspire guests to become involved in the preservation of the Mansion and other historic sites.

The American Women's Heritage Society has sponsored numerous significant exhibitions during its ten-year history. For the "We the People 200" celebration which commemorated the signing of the United States Constitution in September 1987, the "Life in the Colonies for Black Freed Men and Women"

Figure 18/19: Belmont Mansion complex exterior renovations

Figure 20: Belmont Mansion complex banquet room after restoration

Figure 21: Belmont Mansion complex sitting room after restoration

Figure 22: Belmont Mansion complex atrium before amd after restoration

Figure 23: Opening of the holiday season with lighting of the candles by Kofi Asante, Father Gregory Smith, Monsignor Gibbons and Rabbi Aaron Lanslo

Figure 24: A Christmas Carol play at Belmont

exhibit recreated the lives of historically documented 18th and 19th century African-American Philadelphians through furnished interiors at Belmont Mansion. This exhibit displayed the living room of James and Charlotte Forten, wealthy Abolitionists; the bedroom of Matthew and Sarah Heath, a skilled carpenter and his dressmaker wife; and the kitchen of Robert and Phoebe Hill, a porter and washerwoman. This event was also celebrated by the performance of a re-enactment "Black Women of the Constitution" by actors from the Bushfire Theater Company.

Also in 1987 the Society displayed "Black Women: 200 Years of Contributions to the City of Philadelphia," an exhibit of commissioned portraits by renowned artist Sam Byrd of African-American women from Philadelphia who made significant contributions to the arts, education, law, politics, and medicine. In 1988 the "Yunlan He: Chinese Art Exhibit" featured the unveiling of Yunlan He's portrait of W. Wilson Goode, Mayor of Philadelphia. The portrait was presented on the occasion of the Mayor's birthday. This exhibit was followed in 1989 by the "Black Folk Dolls: A Journey to the Past" exhibit, accompanied by a lecture.

In September 1989 the Tri-centennial Celebration of Belmont Mansion was celebrated by a gathering of forty-four descendants of William and Richard Peters, the original owners of Belmont Mansion (Fig. 26). A special feature of this event was an exhibition of Peters family paintings, photographs, and artifacts loaned by family members. During this event, the City Council of Philadelphia passed a resolution honoring the American Women's Heritage Society for restoring and maintaining Belmont Mansion. In 1991 the Society celebrated

Figure 25: Tri-Centennial Celebration - Board Members and President

Figure 26: The decendents of William and Richard Peters Family who gathered at Belmont Mansion for the Bicentennial Celebration

Figure 27: Eartha Kitt and the President at "Back to Belmont" Campaign Benefit Concert with American Womens's Heritage Society President Audrey Thornton-Johnson

*Figre 28: African American Womens
in the Military Exhibit*

*Inside Hatfield House
Africa Oye Exhibit*

Figure 29: African-American Women in the Civil War Exhibit

its Fifth Anniversary at Belmont Mansion with a Colonial Costume Ball. Performances of 18th and 19th Century dances and chamber music were the highlights of the evening.

Exhibits celebrating Black History Month and Women's History Month have been an annual highlight at Belmont Mansion. In February 1988 the "From Africa to America" exhibit showed the history of the movement of African people to the Americas through slavery. In February 1990 the "Sadie Tanner Mossell Alexander" exhibit paid tribute to the life of this noteworthy Philadelphian who paved the way for African-American women in law. In 1991 the "From Whence We Came: A Tribute to Black Women's Organizations" exhibit showed the importance of local African-American women's groups to the civic life of Philadelphia. In February 1992, the "America's First Native Born Master of Music: Frank Johnson" exhibit brought the contribution of this native Philadelphian to the attention of the community. The "Historical Black Images and Film: Where We Were to Where We Are" exhibit in February 1993 showed how blacks were portrayed in the film and print media in the first half of the twentieth century. The "African-American Women in the Civil War Era" exhibit in March 1994 was complemented by lectures by Dr. Ella Forbes and Dr. Emma Jones Lapsansky. The "Black Women Organized for Social Change, 1800-1920" exhibit in February 1995 explained the contribution of African-American women's social, civic, and religious organizations to education and equality. The "African-American Women in Sports" and "African-American Women in the Military" exhibits in February and March 1998 demonstrated the lasting contributions of African-American women in these fields. At the opening of the "African-American Women in Sports" exhibit, Dawn Staley of Philadelphia's women's basketball team, The Philadelphia Rage, was the guest speaker. Among the women featured in the exhibit was Velma "Baby TNT" Garrick, the first African-American woman to work as a professional boxing referee. In the "African-American Women in the Military" exhibit, among the distinguished women recognized for their service in World War II and for their continued service to our country are Brigadier General Clara Adams-Ender, First African-American Chief of the Department of Nursing at Walter Reed Army Medical Center, Dr. M. Joycelyn Elders, Former Surgeon General of the U.S. Public Health Service, Susan Elizabeth Freeman, Chief Nurse of the First Overseas Unit of Black Nurses during World War II, Dr. Mae C. Jamison, First Female African-American Astronaut, Brigadier General Hazel W. Johnson-Brown, First Female African-American General Chief of the Army Nurse Corp, Brigadier General Carcelite Jordan-Harris, First Female African-American to attain rank of General in the U.S. Air Force, and Janie L. Mines, First African-American Woman at the U.S. Naval Academy.

Another annual event at Belmont Mansion has been the Colonial Christmas Showcase with accompanying musical performances. Performers have included the Fiskites and the School of the Performing Arts. The Society has continued the long history of musical and dramatic performances being held at Belmont Mansion. The dramatic production of "That's Me: An African-American Cultural Experience" was presented in August 1987. In September 1990, musical and dance

Figure 30: Tri-Centennial Celebration at Belmont Mansion

Figure 31: Board of Directors in Colonial Costume

performances by "Africa Oyé" were held at Belmont. In September 1992 the "Jazz Under the Stars" concert featured some of Philadelphia's top jazz artists. In March 1997 the Society held the "Back to Belmont" Benefit Concert, performed by the legendary Eartha Kitt (Fig. 27), to help raise funds for the Belmont Mansion Restoration Project.

The American Women's Heritage Society has always been active in providing programs specifically designed for women and youth. The history of Belmont Mansion and its restoration was featured in the City of Philadelphia School's television series "Geography, History, and the Urban Riches." In July and August of 1995, the Society sponsored an African Arts Summer Youth Program in cooperation with Africamericas for Cultural Development. Tours of an exhibit of African ceremonial masks, drums and other musical instruments complemented lectures and performances of African drumming and dance.

Other special events sponsored by the American Women's Heritage Society have contributed to making Philadelphia the number one destination in America for Minority Tourism. In 1990 a reception for participants in Philadelphia's first Black Memorabilia and Collectibles Show was held at Belmont Mansion. A reception in honor of Prince Nana Akwassi Boakye (Samuel) and Prince Opaku Agyeman, Princes of the Busumuru Faben Stool (Stool of Justice) of the Asante Kingdom of Ghana was held at Belmont in December 1992. In 1994 the Society sponsored a reception honoring the appointment of Mary Mason, talk show hostess and community activist, as a Fairmount Park Commissioner. The Society sponsored a lecture and book the

Figure 32: Belmont Mansion Complex Phase 1

Figure 34a: Opening Reception

Figure 33: Bedroom of the Heath Family in the main building

Figure 33a: Bushfire Theatre Pantomine Actors in main room during 18th Century Exhibition

Figure 35: W. Wilson Goode

Figure 37: AWHS 10th Anniversary Celebration Awardees

Tree Planting Ceremony 1996

signing by restaurateur Barbara Smith in 1995. Other famous attendees of recent events at Belmont include Jesse Jackson and Boyz II Men. Belmont was also the location for the filming of Will Smith's music video "Summertime."

In October 1995 the Society held the "Back to Belmont" Benefit Gala at the Horticultural Center in Fairmount Park while Belmont Mansion was closed for Phase I of the Restoration Project. Honorees, recognized for their contributions to the success of the Society's work at Belmont Mansion, included Mrs. Joseph Gembala, Jr., Past President of Strawberry Mansion; Honorable W. Wilson and Velma Goode, Former Mayor of Philadelphia; William E. Mifflin, Executive Director of Fairmount Park; Harold Murray, Architectural Planner; Honorable Michael Nutter, City of Philadelphia Councilman; Ursula Reed, President of Loudoun Mansion; Honorable Edward Rendell, Mayor of Philadelphia; and Scott J. Schwarz, Esq. of Mattioni, Mattioni, & Mattioni, Ltd. Upon the completion of Phase I of the Restoration Project in June 1997, Philadelphia City Council President John Street presided over the ribbon cutting ceremony for the opening of the Belmont Mansion Complex, at which the Honorable Robert N. C. Nix, Jr. was the special guest.

In addition to exhibits and events sponsored by the American Women's Heritage Society, the Society has thirty member organizations which sponsor their own meetings and events at Belmont Mansion. These organizations include 2000 African American Women, Ain't I A Woman Network, Coalition of African American Cultural Associations, National Association of University Women, Pennsylvania Coalition of 100 Black

Women, Phi Delta Kappa Sorority, Top Ladies of Distinction, Twigs of Montgomery County, and Zeta Phi Beta Sorority.

As the American Women's Heritage Society looks forward to the next decade at Belmont Mansion and the beginning of the new millennium, plans are being made for the future. The Society is actively raising funds for Phase 2 of the Belmont Mansion Restoration Project. The Society will continue to sponsor research on the history of Belmont Mansion, with a special interest in the history of African-Americans and Underground Railroad activities. Ongoing research is being conducted to identify the involvement of Richard Peters in the Abolitionist Movement and his close relationship with the Abolitionist leader Judge William Lewis, his neighbor at Somerton (now Strawberry Mansion).Through interviews with several former residents of Belmont Mansion, the possibility of an underground passageway was discovered at Belmont Mansion. The Society is establishing a library of publications related to the history of Belmont Mansion. An exhibit on the architectural design of Belmont Mansion and its restoration is being developed. Also underway is a furnishings plan for the Belmont Mansion Historic House Museum.

Educational outreach is another area in which the Society is concentrating its efforts. The Society is sponsoring a mentoring program for young women, teaching them about historical research and historic preservation while training them to serve as docents. Educational programs for school groups visiting Belmont Mansion are also under development.

In addition to preserving the historic buildings at Belmont,

Society is involved in preserving the environment. Through the creation of the Belmont Mansion Environmental Education Trail, the Society will provide hands-on experiences in methods for restoring and maintaining natural resources. The Society is also recruiting and training guides to teach visitors about natural resources and the history of human alterations of the environment surrounding Belmont Mansion. As always, fundraising is essential for supporting the Society's educational, research, and preservation programs at Belmont Mansion.

Conclusion

The history of Belmont Mansion and its owners reflects the early history of Philadelphia and the United States of America. During the Colonial era, William Peters built Belmont Mansion as a country estate to be used as a show place for the new family and elevated social status he had acquired in America. The use of Belmont Mansion in the Early American period took a new direction under the ownership of William's son, Richard Peters. Belmont became a retreat for Richard's fellow patriots, George Washington, John Adams, Thomas Jefferson, and many more. Richard put the land to practical use in his agricultural experiments. He also supported the abolition of slavery in public and at home, where he freed the former slave, Cornelia Wells.

After Richard's death, the commercial and industrial development of the Belmont estate was halted when the site was incorporated into Fairmount Park in 1868. For over a century, Belmont Mansion alternated between periods of abandonment and use as a restaurant. At last the historical and architectural significance of Belmont Mansion is being recognized and shared with the public through the work of the American Women's Heritage Society.

The American Women's Heritage Society has shown what can be accomplished when a group of dedicated women interested in history see a need to take charge. The spirits of the past have inspired these stewards of the present to rescue Belmont Mansion from abandonment and neglect. Once again, as in the days of Judge Peters, Belmont Mansion is filled with activity and life. Today, however, it is no longer a refuge for the privileged few. Belmont Mansion is the crown jewel of Fairmount Park, a show place for all Philadelphians that is open for the enjoyment of the entire community.

Historic Hatfield House

MARTIN J. ROSENBLUM, R.A. & ASSOCIATES

BELMONT MANSION: MAIN BUILDING

CONJECTURAL ORIGINAL FRONT ELEVATION

THE HONORABLE RICHARD PETERS
(1744 - 1828)

THE PETERS FAMILY;
descendents of William and Richard Peters
1991

Mr. Ralph F. Peters
Stockton, NJ

Mr. Thomas Richard Butler
Newtown Square, PA

Mrs. Margaret Peters Mathews
Devon, PA

Mrs. Janet Peters Hawley
Devon, PA

Mrs. Charles Conyngham Hawley Hannum
Media, PA

Mr. Richard Peters III
Charlottesville, VA

Mrs. Hope Peters Henry Hill
Sonora, CA

Mr. Richard Hall Henry
Bethesda, MD

Mrs. Edith Wehle
New York, NY

Mr. Arthur Peters
Carrollton, TX

Ms. Agnes Peters
Sharon, CT

Mrs. Verda McQuirk Peters
Eureka Springs, AR

Mr. Churchill Crittenden Peters
San Francisco, CA

Mrs. Claire Taft Peters Johnson
Sequin, WA

Mrs. Marsk Jablonko
San Francisco, CA

Miss Olemaru Peters
Redmond, WA

Mrs. Theodore L. Eliot Jr.
Sonoma, CA

Mr. Sidney VanWyck Peters Jr.
Scotts Valley, CA

Mr. Henry Holman Ketcham
Seattle, WA

Mr. William Peters Ketcham
Seattle, WA

Mrs. Janet Wright Ketcham
Seattle, WA

Mr. George Black Jr.
Naples, FL

Mr. John Y. Huber IV
Scottsdale, AZ

Mrs. Janette Thompson Black Kroenke
Malvern, PA

Mrs. Elizabeth Anchutz Black Voigt
Rosemont, PA

Mrs. Helen Pew Black Mushrush
Westchester, PA

Mrs. Bryan Hamilton Black Yarnall
Westchester, PA

Mr. J. Howard Pew Black
Marlborough, MA

Mr. Argyle Ross Parsons Jr.
Marietta, GA

Mrs. Everett Mitchell
Asheville, NC

Mr. Douglas VanNess Parsons
Darlington, SC

Mrs. Martin Victor
Glen Cove, NY

Mr. John Platt Hubbell Jr.
Chestnut Hills, WA

Mr. Ralph Peters Hubbell
Chazy, NY

Mr. Roger Wolcott Hubbell
Washington, DC

Mr. Richard Grandin Hubbell
Rockport, TX

Mrs. Samuel Urfer
Naples, FL

Mrs. Richard Irons
Naples, FL

Mrs. John Wright
Norwalk, CT

Mr. Ford Wright Jr.
Alexandria, VA

Mrs. Edward Bailey Bilbrey
Rockwood, TN

Mrs. Dorsey Brewer
Columbia, SC

Mrs. Pauline Bailey
Asheville, NC

Mrs. Daniel Bailey Moore
Cashiers, NC

Mrs. Ronald Bailey Sprinkle
Haymarket, VA

Mrs. Molly Conway Butler Swanton
Aspen, CO

Mrs. Anthony Parson Lewis
Darlington, SC

Mrs. Randolph Dun Rosier
Naples, FL

Mrs. Reginald Parsons Heinitsh
Brevard, NC

Mr. John Dun Lechler
Naples, FL

Mrs. Nancy Dun Eckler
Lakeland, FL

Mrs. Lawrence Remmel
New York, NY

Mrs. William McGrail (Tina)
Martine Peters Victor
Oyster Bay, NY

Mrs. Amy Robinson
Londonderry, VT

Mrs. Melvin Arnold
Pepper Pike, OH

Mr. Michael Maher
Manhasset, NY

Mr. Ralph F. Peters Jr.
Carlisle, PA

Mr. Melvin W. Peters
Plainsboro, NJ

Mrs. Dewitt Armstrong
Alexandria, VA

Mrs. Kevin Martin
Lovettsville, VA

Mrs. Edward Johnson Peters Jr.
Jackson, MS

Mrs. Edward Cole
Atlantic, Iowa

Mr. Thomas Peters
Des Moines, Iowa

Mr. Richard Braxelton Peters
Great Falls, VA

Mr. John Carter Peters
Harlingen, TX

Mr. George Lindsay Peters
Shawnee, OK

Mr. Edward Joslyn Peters
Jackson, MS

Mrs. Stephen Aylestick
Great Falls, VA

Mr. Mark Edward Peters
Great Falls, VA

Mr. David Carter Peters
Harlingen, TX

Mrs. Robert Shurden
Wichita, KS

Mrs. Margaret Drennan Hawley
Devon, PA

Mrs. Nellie Peters Rucker Walter
Carauret, MA

Mrs. Ralph Peters Black Jr.
Atlanta, GA

Mrs. John Y. Huber III
Gladwyne, PA

Mr. George Black
Hilton Head Island, SC

Mr. Lamar Cobb Walter
Savannah, GA

Mr. Henry A. Walter Jr.
Richardson, TX

Mrs. Wade H. Boggs III
Atlanta, GA

Mrs. David Gilbert
Smyrna, GA

Mrs. Susan Mather Black
Atlanta, GA

Mrs. Caroline Browne Huber
Houston, TX

Mrs. Philippa Campbell Wehle
New York, NY

Mr. William Peters
San Jose, CA

Mrs. Carolyn Peters
Juneau, AL

Mrs. Michael Warstinske
San Francisco, CA

Mrs. Kathryn Strong
Seattle, WA

Mr. Sam Ketcham
Somerville, MA

Mr. Wilmer Peters
Chesapeake, VA

Mr. Ralph Peters Hawley
Devon, PA

Mr. Smedley D. Butler III
Redding, CT

Mrs. David Schaiger
Glendale, CA

Mr. Theodore Eliot III
Hong Kong

Mrs. Rene Mariani
Bainbridge Island, WA

Mr. James Howell
San Juan Island, WA

Mrs. Michael Fitzgibbon
Olympia, WA

Mr. Peter Eliot
New York, NY

Ms. Debra Peters Mitchell
Shawnee, OK

Mr. Sam Peters
Irving, TX

American Women's Heritage Society Inc., the ...ship for Belmont Mansion, Belmont Mansion Drive • Fairmount Park • Philadelphia, Pennsylvania 19131

Figure 38: Peter's Family decendents

Fig. 40: Plateau hitching rail - view looking north east, scenery in Fairmount Park

Fig. 41: Carriage Sheds at Belmount Mansion, view looking south -west

Fig. 42: Belmount Judge Peters' farm in Charles S. Keiper, Fairmount Park and the International Exhibition at Philadelphia 1876

Fig. 43: Belmount Mansion - Fairmount Park Girard Pension Fund, published 1913

Fig. 44: Sheep grazing on Belmont Plateau Fairmount Park, Girard Pension Fund 1913

Bibliography

Primary Sources

Anthony Wayne Papers, Historical Society of Pennsylvania.
Belmont Mansion, Fairmount Park Commission Archives.
Boelsen House, Fairmount Park Commission Archives.
Edward Carey Gardiner Collection, Historical Society of Pennsylvania.
Miscellaneous Manuscripts Collection, University of Pennsylvania.
Pennsylvania Abolition Society Papers, Historical Society of Pennsylvania.
Peters Family Papers, Historical Society of Pennsylvania.
Philadelphia Society for Promoting Agriculture Papers, University of Pennsylvania.
Richard Peters Correspondence, Cadwalader Collection, Historical Society of Pennsylvania.
Samuel Breck Papers, Historical Society of Pennsylvania.
Roberts Vaux Papers, Historical Society of Pennsylvania.

Secondary Sources

Basalik, Kenneth J., 1991. *Field Report of the Archaeological Investigations at Belmont Mansion.* North Wales, PA.

Black, Nellie Peters, 1904. *Richard Peters: His Ancestors and Descendants.* Atlanta.

Blockson, Charles L., 1994. *Hippocrene Guide to the Underground Railroad.* New York.

Butler, Olivia A., 1994. "Judge Richard Peters and African Americans: An Anatomy of Relationship, 1744-1828." Unpublished manuscript in the American Women's Heritage Society Library.

Butler, Thomas Richard, 1954. "Belmont Through the Years." Remarks delivered at the Numismatic and Antiquarian Society of Philadelphia Meeting.

Campbell, William Bucke, 1942. "Old Towns and Districts of Philadelphia." *Philadelphia History* 4 #5: 93-148.

Cummings, Hubertis, 1944. *Richard Peters: Provincial Secretary and Cleric.* Philadelphia.

Downing, A. J., 1844. *A Treatise on the Theory and Practice of Landscape Gardening, Adapted to North America.* New York.

Finkelman, Paul, 1985. *Slavery in the Courtroom: An Annotated Bibliography of American Cases.* Washington.

Halpern, Martha [no date]. "The Dining Pavilion at Belmont Mansion." Unpublished manuscript under Belmont Mansion in the Fairmount Park Commission Archives.

Halpern, Martha, and John McIlhenny, 1983. "John Boelsen's House and Garden." Unpublished manuscript under Boelsen House in Fairmount Park Commission Archives.

Ives, Amy Cole, 1996. "Belmont Mansion, A Conditions Survey of the Ornamental Plaster Ceilings of Room 101 and 205." University of Pennsylvania M. A. thesis.

Knight, Franklin, ed., 1847. *Letters on Agriculture from His Excellency George Washington, President of the United States.* Washington.

Lemanowicz, Richard J., and Maria F. Ali, 1996. "Belmont Mansion Cultural Landscape Inventory." Unpublished manuscript under Belmont Mansion in the Fairmount Park Commission Archives.

Presser, Stephen B., 1978. *A Tale of Two Judges: Richard Peters, Samuel Chase, and the Broken Promise of Federalist Jurisprudence.* [Chicago].

Rice, Howard C., Jr., 1963. *Travels in North America in the Years 1780, 1781 and 1782 by the Marquis de Chastellux.* Chapel Hill, NC.

Rosenblum, Martin Jay, & Associates, 1992. *Belmont Mansion Historic Structures Report.* Philadelphia.

Scharf, J. Thomas, and Thompson Westcott, 1884. *History of Philadelphia. 1609-1884.* Philadelphia.

Still, William, 1872. *The Underground Railroad.* Philadelphia.

Watson, John F., 1899. *Annals of Philadelphia, and Pennsylvania, in the Olden Times,* vol. 1. Philadelphia.

Westcott, Thompson, 1877. *The Historic Mansions and Buildings of Philadelphia.* Philadelphia.

List of Illustration